"Sarah Smith Ducksworth's poetry collection ...is about identity, perseverance, and the human spirit. ...What's most powerful is the authenticity and confidence of the speaker's voice and the striking figurative language that evokes a mostly bygone era in the American South. Readers nostalgic for this particular time and place and those seeking an uplifting and reflective read will land gently here."

—*Blue Ink,* June 2015

"A voice that is both confident and self-aware makes this a brave and comprehensive poetry collection. Throughout this book of poetry, the speaker is able to reflect wisely on specific events or experiences and transform them into their own unique voice, one that acknowledges the poems' larger meanings in the present moment. Very little is spared in Ducksworth's writing... There are semblances of blank verse, image poetry, and even a few haiku, all of which provide an engaging array of poetic voices. Ducksworth builds a staircase of personal reflections and experiences, none of which are excluded from the whole, and all of which fits into it."

—Kenny Jakubas, *Foreword,* June 2015

"...this collection of poetry is a personal response to the times and nature of Ducksworth's world. With the power of her words, this woman takes us on a journey into her psyche in a manner that illuminates not only her life but all lives. These poems embrace the joy, horror, laughter and sorrow of lives deeply lived, which ultimately becomes the pact we make with the universe and/or God. In words accessible to everyone, this poet titillates, humors, and haunts. The tone and attitude of her poems seem well suited to their language..."

—Diane Elliott, *U.S Review of Books,* January 2015

"Reading Ducksworth's poems, you experience a life that was filled with uneven stairs, hard to climb, broken in spots, but that continued up, so that with enough work, dedication and faith, it was possible to keep climbing to the top."

—Barbara Rybolt, *Independent Press,* April 2015

Chimes of Time

Sarah Smith Ducksworth

Copyright © 2017 Sarah Smith Ducksworth.

Formerly entitled No Crystal Stair

All rights reserved. No part of this book may be reproduced, stored, or transmitted by any means—whether auditory, graphic, mechanical, or electronic—without written permission of the author, except in the case of brief excerpts used in critical articles and reviews. Unauthorized reproduction of any part of this work is illegal and is punishable by law.

ISBN: 978-0-9991586-0-9 (sc)
ISBN: 978-0-9991586-1-6 (e)

Library of Congress Control Number: 2017951070

Lotus Flower Press
1029 Mountain Avenue
Berkeley Heights, New Jersey 07922
973-524-2922
Sarah Smith Ducksworth

Because of the dynamic nature of the Internet, any web addresses or links contained in this book may have changed since publication and may no longer be valid. The views expressed in this work are solely those of the author and do not necessarily reflect the views of the publisher, and the publisher hereby disclaims any responsibility for them.

Any people depicted in stock imagery provided by Thinkstock are models, and such images are being used for illustrative purposes only. Certain stock imagery © Thinkstock.

Lulu Publishing Services rev. date: 10/23/2017

DEDICATION

Ordinary people who spend their lives paving paths for others to follow, do not often leave behind monuments of granite or stone. They build character in the hearts and minds of those they mentor and touch with kindness. And, when they die, they leave the world a better place. Among such unsung heroes, who unselfishly serve humanity and make sacrifices so that others may excel, I count my parents, Clarence Sidney and Lola Kersh Smith. For the many blessings they bestowed on me while they were on this earth, and for the most precious gift of all—life itself—I dedicate this book of heart-felt poems.

Contents

REFLECTIONS 1
1. "Transient Moments" 3
2. "Blackberry Picking" 6
3. "Decatur Street" 9
4. "Ostentatious Easter Sundays" 16
5. "Extended Family: A Bridge Between Them" 18
6. "Hurricane Camille" 20
7. "Why I Ain't Scared of No Iron Claws and No Dracula and Nobody Else I See in the Movies" 22
8. "Daddy Clarence" 27
9. "Her Last Day" 32

REALITY 35
10. "Saphira's Secret" 37
11. "He Don't Wanna Do Right If It Means Living Without The Hands" 41
12. "The Sound Of A Breaking Heart" 43
13. "House By The Railroad Track" 44
14. "Opposing Worlds" 47
15. "Missed Flight" 48
16. "The Leveraging Power of Hate" 50
17. "What a Worldly-wise Man Said to Me, And the Mysteries of Life I Have Pondered" 51

18. "A Ticking Bomb" 54
19. "Another Reason" 56
20. Haiku #1 59
21. Haiku #2 60
22. Haiku #3 61
23. Haiku #4 62
24. Haiku #5 63
25. "Shunners are Hypocrites" 64
26. "Robert Burns" 65
27. "The Angry Beast" 66

RENACENCE 69
28. "What Shunners Intended For Evil Turned to Good" 71
29. "Freedom" 72
30. "Words" 73
31. Solitude 1 74
32. Solitude 2 76
33. "In Your Embrace" 77
34. "At the Breakfast Table" 78
35. "On Writing a Poem" 81
36. "The Quest For Perfection" 83
37. The Enigma of Life: What I Do Not Understand, I Must
    Believe 84
38. "First Day of Class" 86
39. The Reading Autobiography of an English Teacher 89

Reflections

1
"Transient Moments"

Upon a tiny speck of dirt,
An infinitesimal fraction of an atom,
On the sleeve of Infinity,
My destiny was writ.
Intimations of my birth came
In the primordial rising of tides
And in the fiery burst of suns
More ancient than living cells.

After countless transformations, rebirths and transitions,
I awoke upon this Earthly stage
Configured human, female and black,
Destined to spend a predetermined time.

And now, aware that these transient moments
Of life have been nearly spent,
My soul cries out for meaning.

I hear the deep baritone
Of Grandpa Irving Kersh,
Invoking God Almighty
To extend his wonderful blessings
To me, victim of avarice and scorn;
And, as I hunger and thirst for righteousness,
To fill the vessel of my being to overflowing.

Sarah Smith Ducksworth

I smell the ripeness of figs
Plucked from Grandma Sarah's mammoth tree,
Standing sentinel in the backyard of my childhood,
Spreading supple branches laden with fruit and furry leaves
Under the blaring sun of the Mississippi sky.
In its offering of shade and fruit
Was the false promise of safe haven
And intimations of my own womanhood, maturing in season.

I am reminded of the labors and caveats of my parents,
Who, in times of searing oppression,
Taught school in fall and winter
And picked cotton in spring and summer
To make ends meet,
While adhering to Jim Crow laws.
From them, I discovered my own ambition
And forged a practical philosophy:
Education uplifts, even in a cotton field;
Hard work leads to survival;
Life is not fair.

My identity has been solidly cast in fields of ash—
Flesh of my flesh--
And in the red clay of rural Mississippi landscapes—
From dust to dust returnest--
Parched and cracked by relentless summer heat,
Drenched by sudden storms defying the sun
As it refuses to vacate the sky
Or be quenched by clouds and raindrops.

In rivulets of rich red mud,
In reflections of pine trees in muddy waters,
Manifest blood of my blood and bone of my bone.

In 1985, this Mississippi rural dirt road seemed
untouched by the modern world since 1950

Photo permission courtesy of Sheila Ducksworth, photographer (circa 1985)

2
"Blackberry Picking"

I walked deliberately and cautiously
Into that wild terrain,
A mile beyond my uncle's barn and berth,
To a place uncultivated and untamed,
Nourished and cradled by Mother Earth.

Beyond the brush and the bramble,
I tread and I ambled,
Avoiding thorns and other hazards,
Not knowing exactly where to turn
To find dark, sweet, succulent treasures,
Dew drenched in the early morn.

By luck and by savvy,
I found the mother lode: a bevy
Of berries sitting in a surprising clearing—
Wonderful perfection, huge and sweet,
Delicious for snacking and cobbler inspiring.
An awesome treat, impossible to beat.

Into my gallon bucket of tin,
I dropped firm, sweet berries in.
For nearly an hour, I did not quit.
When the fruit crested at the bucket's top,
And a single new berry could not be fit,
I knew it was the time to stop.

As I ceased berry picking,
I heard behind me something swishing.
I did not know if it were friend or rake;
So I made a turn to see
What the cause could possibly be.
That's when I saw this big old snake,
Slithering in a narrow path
And heading straight for me.

I quickly grabbed my blackberry bucket;
And, with great force, I launched it.
With the perfection of a magical trick,
It landed on the snake's flat head;
And I finished the job with a handy stick.

Though I was very saddened to see
The agile reptile lying dead,
I did not regret the dirty deed.
Sir Snake was certainly a sneaky foe,
And it was him or me that had to go.

Berries, berries were strewn here and there,
Scattered practically everywhere.
But spilling berries was not my worry;
I left God's country in a hurry.
I was finished picking for the day,
Stomping on berries along the way.

Sarah Smith Ducksworth

3

"Decatur Street"

Decatur Street children, like my sisters and me,
Roughed it throughout the fifties.
Digital conveniences we enjoy today
Were then products of our fancy—
Ethereal dreams for passing time away.

Black and white TV was our cutting edge—
Broadcasts were on two channels.
Computers were huge machines in labs,
And telephone landlines had to be shared
With two or three parties contending for time
On one very busy transmission line.

However, what we did not have, we surely did not miss.
We made do with what we had.
Using common tools and natural frills,
We made beautiful and complicated things
And named our grand inventions
After our grand intentions.

I made wedding cakes from plain red clay
And used wild flowers to decorate.
I held funerals for beetles and frogs,
Spoke sermons for their absolution,
As I consigned their souls to Heaven,
Using high-sounding phrases and Biblical allusions.

Of course, I was not alone
In making up fun and games.
I had sisters and plenty of playmates,
Who had big ways of thinking.
And, when we got together
In the middle of the street,
We had plenty private space
In which to gather and perform our feats.

A ridiculous game we loved to play
Was: "I lost my handkerchief yesterday
And found it today!
It was all so full of money
That I throwed it away!
Throwed it away!"

First there was a player
Who drew the shortest straw;
And, according to the lottery rule,
Received the booby prize—
A snotty old handkerchief
Which could not be disguised.

Her pick made her an outsider,
Unacceptable to the rest.
And her fate caused her to wander
Outside the ring of friends,
Accepting of the fact that just one thing
Could make her nightmare end.

She would have to be ruthless
In doing what she had to do:
Spot the most careless fellow
To give the handkerchief to.

So she looked for an easy target
As she trudged around the track—
Someone who might not see the missile
When it landed behind her back.

At the first opportunity
To throw the handkerchief away,
The outsider had her chance
To make a brand new day.

But her target was now a pursuer,
Carrying the dirty rag.
And the tosser had to be swift enough
To avoid the other's tag.

Only if she won the race,
Would she be welcomed by the clan
And invited to stay connected
As a member of the band.

But the retriever of the handkerchief
Had no honorable choice.
For, if she lost the furious race,
She became the new outcast,
Teased by everybody for coming in last.

Another racy game we used to play
Required a ring of clappers,
And little Sally Walker
Sitting in a saucer,
Awaiting her chance to be a dancer.

"Rise, Sally Rise!
Wipe your weeping eyes!
Put your hands on your hips
And let your backbone slip.
Now shake it to the East;
Now shake it to the West;
Now shake it to the one that you like the best!"

The most dangerous game we ever played,
We called "Chase the Mosquito Man!"
Of course, we played this game
Without parental permission
And without the old folks' supervision.

The object of this perilous game
Was first: to make ourselves invisible,
Inside the spiraling white bubble
Mosquito Man piped from under his truck;
And then: to search inside the cloud.
For little friends who laughed out loud.

So whenever we saw Mosquito Man coming,
We waited for village keepers
To retreat from yards and porches
And shield themselves inside of houses.
Then once we saw the coast was clear,
We'd rush inside the poison mist
Like musketeers who have no fear.

Mosquito Man's truck was quite compact,
With a very small cab for sitting
And two small windows, kept tightly shut,
To exclude the thick, white vapors—
The sweet-smelling, feel good cloud.

Chimes of Time

Mosquito Man visited our street
Several days of every week,
Especially in July and August
When summer heat almost cooked us
And burly mosquitoes tried to eat us.

Once we entered the thick white cloud,
It was hard for us children to see
Our hands before our faces.
Yet, we could make out shadows of shrouded friends
And tagged as many as we could
Before the light of day returned
To take the mist away.

After a season of foggy fun,
The next summer the game was done;
And Decatur Street children took shelter
Until Mosquito Man completed his run.

I can't remember why the game ended
In the abrupt way that it did;
But I am sure some old fogey
Was the one to close the lid.

Well, I knew all along that a kerosene fog
Was poison to mosquitoes.
But since my friends and I were not insects,
I gave its potency no respect.
Besides, I felt we were super armed,
And I truly thought our lives were charmed.

One day, as I sat sheltered from the fog,
I had a novel thought—
If science is as right as it seems to be,
And all living things are linked on a chain,
Why would not a mosquito killing cloud
Be also a bane to me?

Following this epiphany,
I posed another query—
Was Decatur Street just a convenient default
To halt mosquitos at the color line,
Which separates Mosquito Man's world from mine?

Chimes of Time

Photo (2010) This is the house in which the poet grew up

A section of Decatur Street. (The street still has the look of the 1950s. Only modern cars and new generation residents update it.)

4
"Ostentatious Easter Sundays"

I recall the bygone days of my youth,
When TV shows broadcast in black and white;
And perishables kept cool on blocks of ice;
And every task was a physical chore.
Life in those days could be very drear,
But we had holidays to bring us cheer.

Easter Sunday was my favorite day;
It was filled with much pomp and circumstance.
It was a day for showing style
While strutting in a gay parade
Or acting in a spectacle on stage.

On Easter Sunday I was chic.
I wore an organdy or satin dress
With ruffles, frills, and beads of pearls.
I also wore little white gloves
And fastened on fancy silk bows
To accentuate my Shirley Temple curls.
I sported shoes of patent leather
To offset lacy white socks, ankle high.
No one could tell me I wasn't fly.

Though I was puffed up in Easter finery,
Beside Mother Nature, I surely paled.
Her style was much more ostentatious,
More exuberant and stunningly brilliant.

Easter Sunday dressed in living clothes,
A skirt of velvet verdant grass
Trimmed by multicolored flowers
And flanked by blue skies and budding trees.
No material manufactured to adorn
And no painting of Paradise on canvass
Could ever match her celebration of life reborn.

5

"Extended Family: A Bridge Between Them"

(When William would meet his Grandpa
Bart on a bridge a long time ago)

Between the sightless old man's cabin
And his grown son's new farm house,
Edging forty acres of fields and pine tree forest,
There was a flowing stream of separation—
A ribbon of running water
With pearl white pebbles on the ground beneath
And blue and yellow wild flowers dancing on its banks.

Across the several yards width of flowing waters,
Spanning the length of many miles,
An old plank bridge gently arched;
And rough-hewn wooden railings, smoothed by time,
Curved along the sides,
Creating a beautiful, safe passageway
Between the old man's cabin yard
And his grown son's modern home.

Each day the old man left his cabin at noon,
Carrying his walking stick;
And when he arrived at the foot of the bridge,
He tapped the wood with the tip of his cane.

And the sound, that came from a wooden plank,
Gave him inner-sight and confirmation.

When the old man's doting grandson,
A ten year old growing weed,
Saw his Paw Paw fast approaching
Upon the wooden bridge,
He ran with joy and zest to greet him.
And, to save the old man from accidental harm,
Very gently the little boy
Took his Paw Paw by his frail and ready arm.

6
"Hurricane Camille"

As we sat on the veranda after breakfast
Looking out upon our great planet,
The brilliant day presented a perfect painting
Of Nature in all Her splendor.

Nothing seemed as faultless
As the azure sky
And the velvet green earth,
Perfumed by roses, gladiolas and magnolias.

Into this magnificent scene,
Created by a designer of indefinable talent,
A still, unnatural Motionless insinuated.
It came as quietly as a stalking cat.

We first noticed the air stiffen around us.
Then suddenly we realized
There were no butterflies or bees
Drinking in the nectars of flowers fully flayed and accepting.

We walked around the house,
Arriving at the chicken yard
In time to see chickens go into the barn.
Didn't chickens know it was still mid-morning?

As we wondered, the sky turned gray,
And a cool deceptive wind
Vibrated all green growing things
Down to a single blade of grass,
Gently urging the entire landscape to slow dance.

The sudden change of weather
Gave us a sudden thrill.
But, as the wind grew stronger and the dancing grew wilder,
We rushed inside to escape the cha cha cha
Of the hip shaking mama named Camille.

7

"Why I Ain't Scared of No Iron Claws and No Dracula and Nobody Else I See in the Movies"

———•———

On a hot day in July,
When fans blew heavy, heated air,
And the sun, high up in the sky,
Spun like a wheel of fire—
Turning in the firmament where
Even birds of prey refused to fly—
My two older sisters and I
Wanted respite from burning up.

So we decided to go to the movies,
Where there was air conditioning
And drama probably worth mentioning
To unlucky friends who would sweat all day
While we stayed cool in a wonderful way.

So we put aside our daily labor,
Drew window shades and closed the door.
We caught the segregated city bus,
Which took us downtown to Farish Street,
A place where stylish colored folks liked to meet
And spend their hard won treasures
On moments of escape and pleasure.

Chimes of Time

We had our choice of colored theaters:
The Alamo or the Amite;
And both were in competition
For all the money we had to spend—
Each welcoming our attendance and showing appreciation,
Each providing what to us were plush accommodations.

So when we reached our destination,
We took the theater tour.
And, as we sweated outside portals
To fictional lands of dreams,
We began our serious discussion
Of posted messages and painted scenes

The Amite was offering a double matinee,
Which promised hair-raising thrills;
For, both Iron Claws and Dracula
Were set to wreak havoc
As depicted on movie bills.

By way of contrast,
The Alamo offered a mushy twofer:
With Shirley Temple on one screen
And Mary Poppins on the other,
Promising that nothing would be more heart-warming
Than a family saved by a nanny;
And nothing would be more charming than a cute little girl,
Singing and dancing with good old Uncle Bill.

Well, we sisters were bold and did not need to be told
That we were made of sterner stuff
Than the mush baked into cream puffs.

Sarah Smith Ducksworth

We decided to get kicks from monster uprisings
Since family movies would offer no surprises.
So we made up our minds to sample the rougher fare;
And we entered the Alamo on a dare.

First, Iron Claws caused my eyes to roll
As he menaced people and knocked them out cold.
His mechanical hand caused them nothing but trouble
As he snatched up big trucks and turned them into rubble.
My heart pounded because nothing seemed fake,
And I longed for Mary Poppins and Uncle Bill
To take away a frightening chill.

Next came the greedy monster Dracula,
Who kept biting people on the neck.
By the middle of this movie,
I was a veritable wreck;
And my lighter-complexioned sisters
Looked blue around the gills.
It was easy for me to see
That neither of us liked our promised thrills.

But, when one of the characters drove a stake
Into the heart of another,
My oldest sister, with fifteen-year-old wisdom,
Stood up and plainly said:
"I know it's hot outside, but I think
I could throw up in this cold sink.
I'd like to leave and get some sun.
I don't think monster watching is very much fun."

I wish I could say my leaving the movies
Ended all my monster troubles,
But Iron Claws and Dracula returned
To interrupt my sleep that night.
And on my trail, both rode and rode;
And I ran from them with all my might
Until my mother turned on the light.

I had to tell her about the monster antics,
Which still caused me to feel frantic.
She said, "I know what you saw looked real.
But pictures on a screen can't hurt you
No matter how scared you feel.
Writers make up stories, which actors perform.
They use their talents to incite alarm.

"You must learn to separate fact from imagination
Because in life you will face real machinations
That will test your mind, your heart and spirit.
And, only by staying grounded in reality,
Will you have the life you merit.
Trust me, for what I say is true.
No figment of a fertile mind
Will ever be able to harm you.

8

"Daddy Clarence"

Our neighbors on Decatur Street
Called my daddy "Professor".
He was an imposing Afro man,
And he was a very sharp dresser.
Standing at six feet two inches tall,
He needn't watch his weight at all.

He taught seventh grade in a rural school,
Coaching country children on mathematical rules.
Since he was not a great disciplinarian,
He complained often about many contrarians.

He drove to work on Monday mornings,
Making a two-plus hour commute.
He wore stiff white shirts, ties and suits;
He donned a hat and carried a tote.
And, when he returned home on Friday nights,
He wore the same attire.
He was always clean, and his clothes looked pressed
After he'd driven a hundred miles without rest.

Daddy Clarence was a man of few words,
Though he listened very closely.
Still, he offered very few opinions
And kept his early life a mystery.
But, if you studied his expression and filled in the spaces,

You would have heard, within the breaches,
Whispers of tender years spent in strife
And felt the impact they left on his life.

My daddy had but one natural eye;
The other one was glass.
Somewhere, somehow, before I was born,
Somebody knocked his left eye out,
Directly from its shallow socket.
A tragic, bloody accident—
Collateral damage, I was told.
And, as the story goes...

Daddy was walking down Farish Street,
Where colored people liked to meet.
He did not suspect that, on a fateful night,
There would be an awful fight
Inside a rib and catfish bar;
And an angry chap caught up in the fray,
Would hurl a coca cola bottle his way.

Despite the tragedy in the tale,
On his loss, he would never dwell.

Daddy Clarence would sometimes complain
That money did not fall down with rain.
But his three spoiled daughters were wasteful,
And we never accepted his explanations
Whenever he tried to set limitations.
Though we had plenty to eat,
We asked for many extra treats.

Chimes of Time

We demanded sneakers and lipsticks and high heeled shoes.
And somehow Daddy always managed
To purchase every superfluous good
We selfishly demanded.

One Christmas Day I cried because I had no toy.
And, despite the feast on the table,
Foolish tears ended Daddy's holiday joy.
So, he went out to find an open store
To buy me a pair of skates and even more.

Throughout his working years,
Daddy dreamed of acquiring, just for himself,
A brand new Cadillac.
But, for a black man teaching in a rural school,
He had a better chance of buying a railroad track.

Opportunity came in disguise in 1965,
When school integration was implemented,
Forcing reorganization and compromise
And Daddy Clarence's retirement.

Contrary to what his children expected,
Daddy Clarence enjoyed his exit,
Which came with a fixed check for service
And even more—I have to mention—
Money from a government pension.

When commuting expenses did not apply,
And, after his grown daughters left with loving goodbye,
He had funds to use at his discretion—
Enough to purchase his caddy with great satisfaction.

For seven years, Daddy Clarence rode in style,
Treating his dream machine like a child.
But life's pressures had taken their toll.
And declining health shortened his time of ease.
Diabetes, high blood pressure and kidney disease
Exhausted his energy and his hope.

After ten years of dialysis…then a stroke,
Daddy Clarence said his life seemed a cruel joke.

As phantom butterflies entered his sick room,
And spirits of ancient family gathered,
He said he believed he was nearing his tomb.
I told him to stop his grim imaginings,
And I promised Daddy Clarence he would be all right
If he could view life in a more positive light.

Daddy Clarence's voice stilled at once.
Then, suddenly, he smiled up at me;
And his gaze became very even.
I felt the flutter of butterfly wings,
As his soul departed to Heaven.

9
"Her Last Day"

The telephone rang;
I hesitated to pick it up.
It had been a long plane ride home from Las Vegas,
Where I had vacationed for a week.
During that time, Mama and I did not speak.

I felt she was fine.
At the age of eighty,
She had a full life
With church, friends
And my oldest sister for a next door neighbor.
Her time for making ends meet was done;
No more hard labor.

Mother and I lived miles and miles apart.
I was east coast and she was deep south.
But we spoke every day.
It was our routine.
She was chatty and funny,
And her mind was keen.

For just one week,
I had broken communications:
How are you today?
And, what's the weather like?
And, did you get the faucet fixed?
And, what's up with Miss Geneva?
Do you think her husband will leave her?

Having left cold New Jersey for a week,
I had basked in desert sun;
And I did some things I'd never done.
Surely, Mama understood.
Surely, no harm in doing that.
So why did I feel so much like a rat?

When I answered the phone and heard her voice,
I began the prelude to our discussion,
"How are you doing, Mama?"
"Fine," she offered, her usual reply.
I always had to ask her more than once
To give her time to shape her response.

Suddenly, she mused with a certain longing,
As explanation for her untimely call,
"I just wanted to hear your voice."
Startled, I did not have a good reply;
"I'm glad you called," is what I said,
"I intended to call you before going to bed."

Next, I asked about her health,
Her favorite topic of any day.
She answered, without listing her aches and pains,
"I feel better than I've felt in a long time," is what she said.
I happily exclaimed, "Mama, that's really good.
I would fly down to celebrate with you if I could."

She said her sinuses were suddenly clear,
And her aching back was very much better.
She had just returned from church,
And considered that taking a nap
Should be her next choice.
"So good to hear your voice..."

Her little nap became sleep eternal.
And, God knows, I really miss her.

REALITY

10

"Saphira's Secret"

Wrapped tightly in Henry's embrace,
Saphira felt uncommonly safe;
And for the moment she forgot,
That loving him was for naught.

For she was trapped by a history,
Which to Henry was still a mystery.
He could not fathom why
Saphira always acted so shy
When signs of love were in her eyes.

He waited patiently for Saphira to yield;
But he did not know the pain behind her shield.

To Henry this woman was the embodiment of perfection.
Proof appeared from every direction.
In her demeanor he saw a spirit,
Which bespoke exceptional merit.
She was indeed both kind and beautiful;
And, toward the poorest of the poor, she was dutiful,
Giving them freely of her small treasure,
And offering help in very good measure.

Henry's love for Saphira grew stronger each day,
Although he wondered what stood in the way
Of her returning to him, in greater part,
The tender feelings of love he sensed in her heart.

Holding her close, he felt Saphira sigh.
Uncomprehending the meaning of her cry,
He uplifted her chin for a kiss
And heard, instead, a serpent's hiss.

With the force of a tiger, Saphira loosened his hold,
Lest the cause of her dismay should begin to unfold.
After setting herself free, she ran as though from fear.
No longer could she bear to have Henry near.

By chance, Saphira found a church with an open door,
And rushed to the altar where she fell to the floor.
Bitter tears stained her cream colored face,
Tinted by the caramel of a despised race.

The scenes of the past returned to her in a rush;
And the silence of years broke like a gush
Of unchained memories
Framed in cinematic reveries.
Suddenly she could plainly see
The cold eyes of the man who took her virginity.

Master Jim had called her his most beautiful slave,
But he took from her what she never gave.
Painfully, she recalled the roughness of his passion
And his callous disdain for her tearful reaction.

Chimes of Time

The child she bore for Master Jim
Was not the spitting image of him.
The baby's face, framed by ringlets of curls,
Was a miniature Saphira, a gorgeous girl.

If beauty is ever counted as a grace by a free race,
In a slave girl, it leads most often to disgrace.
Saphira would not be the instrument of future horror,
So she smothered the child to end its sorrow.

She knew that even God would not understand
What had compelled her awful hand.

The sin of murder tortured Saphira's soul;
So she swore as a penance to grow old
Without taking pleasure in joys manifest,
And to dedicate herself to uplifting the oppressed.

When slavery ended, Saphira walked away,
Though not into a brighter day.
She entered a scene of scholarly preparation,
Intent on paying heavy reparation.

She used her talent as a weaver of lace,
To pay for lessons in literacy and social grace.
She advanced in these arts really fast
Until her intellect and diction became foils to her past.

In time, she began to teach girls of her race;
And they uplifted others while climbing at an even pace.
Saphira kept her promise to always do good,
Refusing to live abundantly as many thought she should.

But Henry had come to offer her a love so rare;
And she was tempted mightily, but she did not dare
To accept from him a more fulfilling life
While the ghosts of her past filled her soul with strife.

How could she give herself to this loving man
And wear his golden wedding band
With a secret so heinous and depraved
She wanted to take it unspoken to her grave?

Her prayer to end her misery was not in vain;
But, instead of Death, a celestial vision came,
Assuring an end to her duress
And promising, for her suffering,
She would be blessed.

Such reassurance that God
Had forgiven her heavily burdened heart
And benevolently washed her sins away,
Gave her peace and hope for a wedding day.

When Saphira uplifted herself from the floor,
She saw dear Henry standing at the church door.
Intuition had already informed his understanding,
And it was not in his soul to be demanding
Confessions to sins that remained unrinsed,
When he knew she was less sinning than sinned against.

As Saphira told Henry about the death of her child, so meek,
He couldn't stop the tears that rolled down his cheeks.
But greater pity and unfailing love he reserved for the living.
He would spend the rest of his life being faithful and forgiving.

11

"He Don't Wanna Do Right If It Means Living Without The Hands"

At the end of his work day,
He wants, needs and receives
Delicate hands:

Thinly veined,
Long tapering fingers,
Smooth pink nails,
Finely patterned palms with long lifelines.

These hands caress, arouse and excite.
They are expert in erotic pleasure.
They are eager manipulators for treasure.
They take more than they give.

Sated and empty handed,
He leaves his palace of pleasure.
Guilty and ashamed but outwardly bold,
He goes home.

Hands at the kitchen stove stir his dinner.
They are worn hands:

Heavily veined,
Short stubby fingers,
Splintered, uneven nails,
Wrinkled palms with long lifelines.

These hands are roughened
By detergents, scouring powders and polishes.
They are thickened
By hard labor and osteoarthritis.
They are gnarled by worry and neglect.

These hands no longer pleasure.
They accuse.

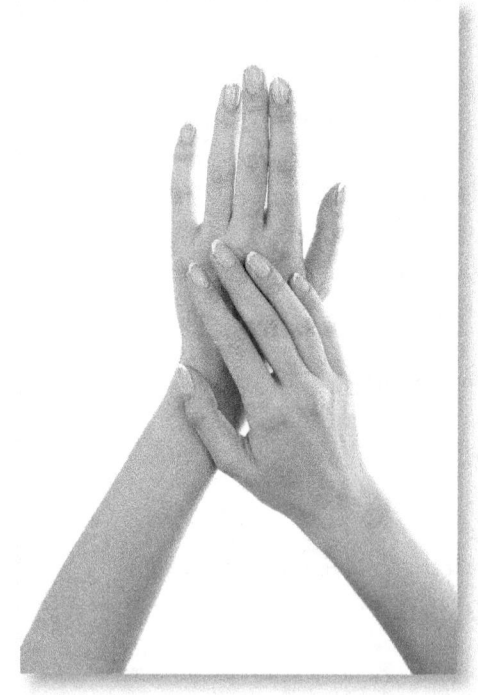

12
"The Sound Of A Breaking Heart"

In a strain of minor notes,
Is the sound of a heart breaking:
Discordant and forlorn,
Penetrating the darkest night,
Knelling under the inane chatter of loons
And the shrieking of cranes.
Decrescendo, it crosses the River Styx
And makes its way to the gates of Hell.

So piteous is the sound of heartbreak
That I sink into despair, and I wonder
What harsh instrument causes such agony.
Can it be love gone awry?
Or the death of a loving mother?
Can it be an enemy's revenge?
Or the betrayal of a bosom friend?

From what I know of the human soul,
It can be the unspringing of hope:
The final fracture of a once precious dream.

13

"House By The Railroad Track"

The house by the railroad track
Sulks like a jilted woman—
A Miss Havisham—
Abandoned by a lover,
Who long ago tended her with loving care,
Decorated her walls with patterned paper,
Cooked meals upon her glowing hearth,
Pumped laughter throughout her many chambers.

Halcyon days of butterflies and rhymes
Are now faint in her memory
And breathlessly fallen into oblivion.
She barely recalls
The taunting beauty of Nature.

Once upon her ample lawns
Spread stout oaks and gay perennials.
They blossomed in spring,
Burgeoned in summer, shed grandeur in fall,
And stood bare in winter under the weight of snow.

Now, all vestiges of that beauty,
Once conceived as eternal,
Is overpowered by the sootiness of coal,
Which drives the future.

Nevertheless, she will not plead for mercy.
She is anchored to that bleak place
Beside the railroad track.
She stares, with hope forlorn, through lintel
windows—
Overdone, overdressed, overly ornate.
She reviles the fickle hands
That deserted her in quest of art nouveau,
A modern mansion, seductive with long lines of urgency.

Still, she is too proud to crumble,
Too stubborn to fall
Upon the steel tracks of progress.
She will not acknowledge the sleek, silver train
Forged by an industrial revolution,
Passing her by without a single salute.

Sarah Smith Ducksworth

14

"Opposing Worlds"

In the model world,
We move as robots
Programmed to behave.
In step, we conform
To rules and regulations,
And tend our obligations.

Parallel to this model world,
Men and women with digital minds
Create chaos.
They bide no rules;
They exude no charm;
They foment only the greatest harm.

Disorder invades my space,
Crushing civility.
Knocking down barriers of privacy,
Obliterating lines once etched in concrete—
Lines that separated whims from rights.

The sons and daughters of Sam high-five,
Proclaiming victory.

15

"Missed Flight"

I received word of my reprieve
While listening to the evening news.
Reporters spoke in grave detail
Of Airline Flight 370.
The mystery of the plane's fate
Kept pundits alert and guessing.

I had a ticket for that flight,
But timing kept me on the ground.
I missed the plane by half an hour,
And cursed myself for being late.

Had I rushed just a little more,
I would have sat in seat Twenty-four.
In the darkness of March Eighth,
I'd have been riding in the sky,
Across South China Sea, soaring high.

However, I would have slept in silent space,
Belted into a leather seat.
But I did not reach the gate in time,
And the plane left me far behind.

Chimes of Time

Now, let's suppose I had got on board—
I would have been calm and collected;
And I don't believe I would have heard
The last good night said to the world—
That final broadcast from the plane
Would have been muted by a snore.
For habit leads me to deep sleep
In sync with cruising altitude.

My eyes may have opened, I think,
When the aircraft spiraled and fell.
But it would have seemed like a dream;
And I hope, hypothetically,
That I would not have had the time
To reason through the confusion
And know that the chaotic intrusion
Was not a nightmarish illusion.

If I had boarded that doomed plane
And become part of the food chain,
I would not be alive today.
A bullet dodger, I am here,
Feeling safe and secure from harm.
Yet in my heart and soul, I know,
Whether traveling in air, at sea, or on land,
My turn will come without reprieve.
My life is in a stalker's hand.

16

"The Leveraging Power of Hate"

It's not love that makes the world go around.
What does it better is hate.
Saint Peter may stand at Heaven's gate,
But he can't get an audience in this town.

It's more fun to hate your neighbor
When you can seize opportunity
To steal the treasures she savors
And destroy her life with impunity.

It is indeed a very good game
To watch her scurry to protect
The home she holds sacred
And the fame she had once attained.
It will be interesting to see
If she survives total neglect
Of all her rights of citizenship
And keeps her marbles and a stiff upper lip.

If you don't like the truth she tells,
Just say her views are manufactured.
And be sure to hammer her well,
As all her dreams become fractured.

Oh, Hate can bring out all the hounds in hell,
And give them thrones on which to dwell.

17

"What a Worldly-wise Man Said to Me, And the Mysteries of Life I Have Pondered"

In the twilight of my life,
I entered a period of strife.
I saw no rhyme or reason
For the coming of this awful season.
I couldn't understand why my life was such a mess,
So I turned to a person who wore the trappings of success
And asked him if an explanation could be inside his head.
Without a blink or hesitation this is exactly what he said:

"The world began with the Big Bang;
And this phenomenon is the one thing
That jumpstarted Evolution,
Which includes physical processes and biological execution.
Extreme molecular motion formed the earth
From which came our bones and flesh.
And all living things born this way will return to Nature's turf.

"Now, man's closest relative is the hairy ape,
But sociology shows us that only man creates red tape,
Producing all the trouble aggravating both you and me
And making life complicated in this greedy society.

"So don't be afraid of any man;
Just try to get all the money you can
And know there is no such place as hell
Where sinful people go to dwell.
Nor is there a heaven to reward suffering and pain.
So, if you want to be a winner while alive on this plain,
Just use every opportunity for material gain.

"No prayers you make to an unseen God
Will make any of your entanglements
Become any better arrangements.
Just go on and do whatever you feel.
Never deny yourself your right to chill.
Your higher power exists only inside yourself,
So put your worries on a fucking shelf.
If you turn the other cheek, you'll just get hit.
You don't have to take anyone's shit,
Or be a sucker tricked out of a dime
By allowing some fucker to beat your time.
If you have enough money, well or ill-got,
You can make up laws to make your enemies rot.
Then your life can be as exciting as you choose.
It can be like playing a game with little to lose."

These words the wise man said to me
Filled my heart with agony.
Science has answers, I had to admit,
That seem to support his argument.
Every tangible thing upon this Earth,
To which humans assign any worth,
Appears to have evolved from unyielding rules
As calculating as math and as solid as tools.

Yet, the more I thought, the argument lost its hold.
I sensed there is more to living well than silver and gold.
My inner Soul then cried out for recognition.
It asked if science could find the site of intuition,
Or prove the existence of truth and beauty,
As well as concepts of love and duty.

I was glad to admit that science has no answers
For such needful and powerful abstractions;
And my Soul delighted in my perceptions
That I am more than the sum total of body parts,
And that the vital sign of life isn't just a beating heart.

I must think again about the mythic scientific,
Which the wise man cited as cataclysmic.
Perhaps the term "Big Bang" is a big misnomer.
For nowhere in the theory is there a hint of a producer,
Or of Big Bang matter igniting without permission
And starting the chain reaction for this earthly condition.
There must have been something behind it all, you see,
And that SOMETHING is what frail humanity can not see.

18

"A Ticking Bomb"

———— • ————

To go to the Greasy Spoon by driving down a dirt road a half mile off the county line road on a Saturday night
To go past Old Palestine Church where saints will meet on Sunday

To arrive at the dirt clearing and park my pickup truck in front of the juke joint
To walk with cross eyed eagerness and gritty anticipation to the devil's nest

To enter the dance hall filled with blue light like fog over the river to hell
To adjust my eyes to shadowy shapes, silhouettes of human beings changed by the dull glow

To consort with sinners and roll with Annie while the getting is good, so good
To dance loose hipped and shoulder rolling to funky, finger popping music

To sit at a table a waiter has prepared for me and eat a catfish sandwich prepared by a cook in a dirty apron
To drown my discomfort in Johnny Walker Red and keep my eyes peeled for anyone wanting to mess with me

To curse the sucker who trips over my left foot which I left sticking out from the side of my table
To explode in anger, stick my switchblade in his throat, and see him fall

To answer your question, *Why?*
To tell you the truth: "He deserved what he got. I got my own problems."

19

"Another Reason"

In his eyes I recognized Evil,
Unfrozen and flashing beneath an infectious smile.
And his cross-eyed look was a dead give-away,
Causing the naïve to pitch and sway
And only the brave to refuse to stay.

Undaunted, I remained mesmerized.
Feeling short of breath and hypnotized,
I heard the devil speaking to me,
Playing upon my vanity,
Promising me good luck and favor
And all the dainties I could savor
If I would join his prosperous team
And participate in all his schemes.

Along with others who stayed
To see his game well played,
I saw the devil's left foot twitch.
And, I knew, don't ask me how,
That his cloven hoof had developed an itch
Inside his slick, polished leather shoe.
And I knew he needed to strike and paw
In darkness far below the blue.

Yet, his right hand kept its cunning,
As he kept on exhorting and promising.
Ah yes, his voice was rich and mellow;
He was such a charming fellow.

My soul, you think, should have been shaken.
But I was instead caught up and taken,
Exported to that foggy land of dreams
Where wealth and power are possible things.
And rules proscribing the heart's desire
Are broken and tossed upon a funeral pyre.

I was determined not to be left out;
So I applauded the devil and gave him a shout.

And now that my eternity is confirmed in hell,
You may wonder why I succumbed to the devil's spell.
You may think it was all for greed,
But if you consider the whole cloth motive for what I did
And think of nothing short of treason,
You may, indeed, see another reason.

20
Haiku #1

Figs ripen in sun,
Turning purple and golden.
June bugs spoil the fruit.

21
Haiku #2

———•———

From hard, bitter seeds
A lonely bonsai tree grows,
Twisted and lovely.

22
Haiku #3

Crickets talk to me
By rubbing their little legs—
Strange conversations.

23
Haiku #4

They wanted to see
If one-legged grasshoppers hop.
They hacked off one leg.

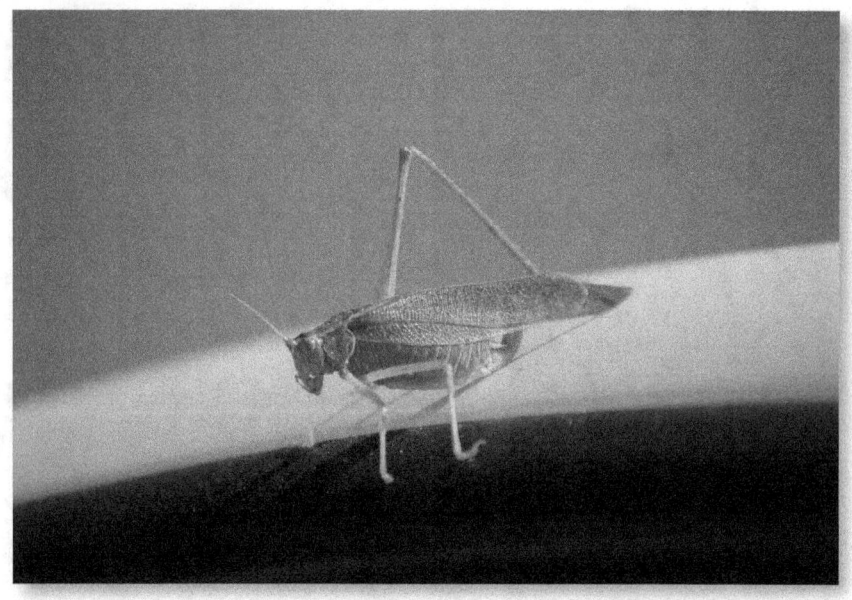

24
Haiku #5

Crystal balls falling
From a cloud-free, friendly sky,
Hail the mystery.

25
"Shunners are Hypocrites"

A reprehensibly evil man
Drags my name through the mud,
And tries to convince other people
That I am a charlatan, pretending to be an intellectual.
He convinces a few, who shun me too;
And, as a pack, they laugh and say I'm a hack.

Yet, they all covet my ideas
And enter my computer to read my honest words,
Which to me, are not very rare;
But they are all I can use
To record my Truth and sing the blues.

26

"Robert Burns"

Sitting at my computer desk,
Bob Burns said to me,
Quietly, but quite emphatically,
"People are no good."

This young man, educated, gainfully employed,
White, and over twenty-one
Became, at once, an enigma to me.
"What," I wondered, "has made him so jaded?"

I wanted to say, "Your assessment is too harsh;"
But there was something in his eyes, so knowing,
That I refrained and sadly agreed.

Since then I have come to realize
That evil lurks even in places reserved for the common good.
It awaits opportunity.
What Bob Burns said was prophecy—
Naked.
And it haunts me still.

27

"The Angry Beast"

In the middle of my life's journey,
I chose, from many possibilities,
A door that led to a garden
Which grew a specific fruit
I hoped to enjoy.

There were other doors,
Leading to other gardens
Bearing different kinds of fruit,
Equally sweet;
But the garden I chose suited me.

The path to that lush and bountiful place,
The object of my desire,
Was rather rough and untamed.
But, with perseverance,
I crossed every hurdle,
Avoided every pit.
Until, in my old age,
I stood looking upon a veritable feast.

However, before I could select
One bright red apple,
I was espied by an angry beast.
Why it was so angry,
I did not know;
But it left tending its own garden
To block mine.

RENACENCE

28

"What Shunners Intended for Evil Turned to Good"

When you turn your back to deny my presence,
And when your eyes scan a small room
But do not acknowledge my face,
And when you ignore merit in the work I do
And give awards and treasures to others of different hue,
I know how much you shun me.

I used to feel neglected and very hurt
Until I learned to get up from the dirt
That you intended for me.

By reclaiming the song that sets me free,
I've found an open door.
And now my spirit soars across the bluest sea,
The tallest mountains and the greenest meadows
And takes rest in a lavender tree.

29

"Freedom"

I have been called a colored person,
a black girl and a negro bitch.
And, I am proud to say,
Such appellations and concepts
have not changed a thing.

God's plan for me has made me what I am.

I am a mother, a wife, a sister, a friend
and a foe.
I am a teacher, a speaker, a creative writer
and a poet.
I am me--
And I am free!

30

"WORDS"

I want my words to engage in dialogue with my soul,
Unlock secrets and define the meaning of my life.

I want my words to be precise,
Honed to the point they can imprint strength and peace
And etch understanding.

I want my words to uplift me
And keep me above the fray.

I want my words to become tools
For building a safe place
Where the past does not haunt me
And the future does not confound me.

In a powerful way,
I want my words to ring truth—
To perpetuate love that is healing
To the human spirit;
Uniting, not dividing,
But expanding joy
And embracing the huge human heart
That beats on one accord.

31

SOLITUDE 1

Like a loose thread yanked
From a tightly woven tapestry,
Joy was ripped from my heart.
And the pattern of my life unraveled
Becoming a heap of disconnected threads.

I used to wallow in self-pity;
My hopes approached a state of atrophy,
And I wondered why Evil had attacked
me so relentlessly.
I wanted it to vanish like an illusion,
Ending seven years of criminal confusion.

In a frenzy of fear,
I saw temples of my creation disappear.
My most sacred beliefs and dreams drew fire
And provided Cyberspace fodder for a funeral pyre.

With raw emotion, I asked the Lord,
"Why hasn't hard work brought me more reward?
Long have I labored gathering forgotten facts
From crumbling archives and historical tombs.
Was it only to see my unmade books
Trapped in unproductive wombs?

What remote hands and twisted minds
Can penetrate space and pierce brick walls
To wrong me so egregiously?"

The answer came quickly while I kneeled.
Suddenly, the whirlwind ceased to reel.

A sanctified voice spoke to me
In a slight ripple of air passing by.
And, in a wave of light, I saw these words:
"Oh, faithful servant, yours is the gain.
The heathens who have authored your pain
Do not heed a living God.
They will die unsaved with unclean hearts.
What phantom hands have done to you
Is something you cannot undo.
Yet, the joy you thought you had lost
Will return to you—free without cost."

And so, I cast aside useless despair
And began to breathe clarified air,
Stored in my soul from a healthier clime,
Long ago provided by the Savior Divine.

Within my mind's eye appeared a new direction
And a simple plan for making correction.

And so, in solitude, I spend my time wisely,
Repairing my broken heart
And building new temples for a brand new start.

32

SOLITUDE 2

Quiet times allow us
To shut down
And shut out
The world,
Where turmoil and pain
Agitate a troubled mind.

In quiet times,
We discover a healing balm
And find safety in angels' arms.

Solitude provides clearer insight.
It highlights salty words of affliction
Flayed in pages of an open book,
Measuring the breadth of our deeds
And the depths of our needs.

We edit rough spots.
We seek golden truth.
We regroup our thoughts and reflect.
We write new text.

33
"In Your Embrace"

When you hold me
I do not think of past, present, or tomorrow
I am flesh undone,
A disembodied soul
Connected to the hum of the Universe
Recorded at the beginning of time
When all things were unmade
And seeking a form to become.

34

"At the Breakfast Table"

Sitting at the breakfast table
Looking through three double paned windows,
We two, wife and spouse,
Bask in the wonder of spring.

Fifty years of our seventy on earth,
We have been a couple,
Never taking for granted
The miracle of spring,
Full sun and April showers,
Transforming winter's wasteland
And our quadrant of the planet,
Teeming with new life.

This morning, a majestic bluebird,
Carrying a bit of twig in its beak,
Dances upon our deck for at least thirty minutes.
We suppose he is enjoying the pristine breaking of the day,
As old Sol Invictus stretches out his arms
And sends down to earth golden shafts of sun, starburst-like.
Sunbeams decorate our dining table as we listen
To the clarion singing of our feathered friend.

Chimes of Time

Between the notes the bluebird sings,
We hear a soprano calling from a distant tree.
Reluctantly, the dancer, prancer, blue bird singer
Dutifully retreats.
We think it leaves to help its mate build a new spring home.

In the wake of its leave-taking,
We remark upon how much we are like a pair of birds.
Only our nest has become empty.
Our little ones have blossomed and flown away.

So, we focus on breakfast: cereal and fruit,
And sip coffee from matching cups.
And soon we begin to reminisce:
We find the solution to the world's ills
Can be reduced to a single grain of sand upon a beach.

We also contemplate, in our morning leisure,
The status of the human condition,
Rehearse the many lessons we have learned,
And list the understandings we have gained
To sustain us when all else has let us down.

I look at you, my old companion, and think:
How curious a pair of keepers we are.
Despite our common love of nature,
We are very different.

You are all logic and detail,
Never jumping to make decisions, good or bad.
You tend our nest because it is practical to do so.
Like the blue bird, you would never neglect or leave me.

On the other hand,
I am all feeling and intuition,
Acting on impulse,
Imagining the whole without considering the parts.
I see what will be lovely in completion,
And I refuse to consider that,
Without building blocks, there is no project.

Fortunately, my dear,
We each catch the other before "divided we fall".
I present to you pearls of imagination, from thinking outside the box.
You present to me the mundane but necessary pieces inside the box.
Like frick and frack we mix and match;
And, through our understanding of what we each bring to life's table,
We re-sew seams in the quilt of our marriage before the fabric separates.

35

"On Writing a Poem"

When I write a poem, I write it all at once.
Yet, it never arrives as a total surprise.
It comes in the service of Truth.
I can only write from what I know.
If I try to impress or write to show
What a genius I think I am,
My would-be poem becomes an awful sham.

In a poem I present my deepest impression,
A segment of life needing my expression.
I will expound upon only one idea
And be daring enough to share it without fear.
In a poem, there is no way I can be insincere,
Or mock values I hold close and dear.

As a photographer uses a few good poses
To depict a wide array of meaning,
From my poetic gleanings,
I select a few clips of memories
From observations of human life.
I try not to skimp on creating emotion,
As I scale heights of both pain and elation.

Through focus and practice in poetic invention,
I have learned first and foremost
That a poem must marry memory and passion;
But the scaffold is the human condition.
When all these considerations converge,
A poem arising from the heart and soul will emerge.

36

"The Quest For Perfection"

All change in elements is orderly,
And Time persists and never ends.
We seek to understand what triggers
the rising tides
And alerts cells, tinier than the eye can see,
To prime their ancient clocks
And to move in sync with celestial spheres,
Tracking the moon as it makes its journey
Across an endless sky.

And I, a speck of dust scattered
by a cataclysmic event,
Am buffeted by care and swaddled in dreams,
Perceiving a cycle inside of myself.
My spirit rotates like the sun in a private space,
My body generates heat as my life burns away.

But, like kindred matter in the universe,
My hot ash will not disappear.
My atoms, released, will make brighter some star;
And my soul will live on to review
The meaning of this earthly journey,
Recording in space, creating eternal verse.

37

THE ENIGMA OF LIFE: WHAT I DO NOT UNDERSTAND, I MUST BELIEVE

I have life.
I breathe;
Sensations assail me;
The wonder of it all compels me,
As I seek meaning in byways
Through which I have meandered.

Now, I ask you…
Is this life just an experiment?
Is it possible it could all be for naught?
If so, why should I struggle?
Why should I even care?
If life is nothing more than "It is what it is",
And if it ends as the severing of a cord,
Why should I care about ragged ends?

Why should I need the temporal love of a friend
If there is no heaven and no hell?
And, why should I fight darkness for an effete light to prevail?

I know no reason to count my blessings
If nothing truly matters.
If my destiny is to be forgotten
Like flotsam tossed upon a river,
I may as well count sheep.

Nothing can impress upon a heart of flesh
That life is everlasting.
If a heart is meat and spirit is fake,
I have no reason to trust in God
Nor to pine for Beauty and Truth.
For Evil and Ugly must last just as long,
And their impact must resound equally strong.

How sad these words sound to me,
I cannot speak them longer.
For, though I do not comprehend life's mysteries,
I can surely recognize the trap of the devil.

Yes, hopelessness is evil,
And melancholy tortures the soul.
Only the never-ending quest for perfection,
Manifest in all of Nature,
Assures me that I won't be forsaken.

God did not make the minuscule cell,
Residing at the bottom of the sea,
To open and shut in perfect time
With the moon when it rises and sinks,
And then allow me to spend my life
In the form of a walking shadow,
Destined to strut and fret
Until my time is spent,
And then be heard no more.

38

"First Day of Class"

I open the door gently
And walk into the large lecture room,
Aware that what awaits me on this date
Is computer generated and sealed by fate.

It is Day One of the semester,
And the room is very crowded.
Unfortunately, I must face this class
With a confidence that is not real.
But no one will ever suspect the jitters that I feel.
For, I'm armed with bold determination
And a firm belief I'll make a good impression.

All eyes stare at me when I say, "Hello",
And echoes return from the few I fondly know.
No other mouths return the greeting
To break the ice of this first meeting.
The silence is like a yawning,
A deep quiet that precedes a dawning.

I say my name and state my business,
Giving this motley crew assurance
That what they see, they'll get;
And that, before the term is over,
They'll have nothing at all to regret.

Still, I am very mindful of the possibility,
I'll be the first black teacher most will have had.
So I decide to let them know that I have earned degrees
That make me subject matter sharp and Michael Jackson "bad".

In a timely way, I tell them of my teaching plan
And how the course will proceed,
With each of them involved in every step
Of textual and literary analyses.
I say that together we will exchange views,
Make use of overt and subtle clues,
And explore socio-cultural contexts
To create multiple meanings equally true.

Once I establish goals within their proximal range,
I know they'll consent to freely exchange
Their names and majors and course expectations.
Growing in comfort, some will reveal their deepest aspirations,
Allowing me to gauge the levels of their engagement
And the amount of study to which they will commit.

The first class meeting moves very quickly;
The end is more relaxed than the start.
Our initial "get acquainted" time has set the tone
To determine how well we'll all get along.
We forge a bridge between us which, in time, will be strong.

Sarah Smith Ducksworth

39

THE READING AUTOBIOGRAPHY OF AN ENGLISH TEACHER

As a teacher, I realize much of what I do in the classroom has been influenced by my own experiences in learning to use language not only as a tool to mediate thought, but also as a source of pleasure.

Both my parents were Mississippi school teachers. Each worked in different counties some distance away from our house in Jackson, the state capital located in the central part of the state.

My father had a very long commute to and from his job. He worked in the Delta region so far north of where we lived that it took him nearly three hours to get to work and the same amount of time to get back home. Of course, this circumstance made it difficult for him to return home every night. So he stayed during weekdays in a boarding house in Belzoni, Mississippi, where his school was located. As a rule, my father came home to his family on weekends.

Fortunately, my mother worked in rural Rankin County in a little town called Brandon, which sits near the Hinds County line where the city of Jackson begins. Back when I was a child, Brandon was less than a half-hour bus ride away; so she was able to commute to work every day and keep home fires burning for her three little girls, including me as the youngest.

Since this was the environment into which I was born, I assumed our lifestyle was the norm. Having a working mom and a weekend dad never fazed me. I never felt abandoned by my daddy, but I clung to my mama. And she gave me almost as much attention as I demanded without allowing me to become unreasonable. My mama had a way of talking to her children that made us want to cooperate and wait for the reward of a good story or a chance to make a pretty picture with paints or crayons. My mama could draw almost anything, and she also could make up stories that would make us laugh at a silly hen or feel sad enough to cry for a crippled child or a starving animal.

Being the baby girl in the family, I had to develop assertive behaviors very early. My two sisters were already in public school by the time I became old enough to see they did not regard me as an ideal companion. Yet, because of their "big sister know-it-all" attitude and their pride in their academic achievements, I was destined to become their child prodigy from the very beginning of my life--but not their favorite playmate. Seeing my sisters do their homework and get Mama's praises for perfectly prepared lessons was inspirational to me. I wanted to hurry up and go to school.

I was two and a half years old when Mama began taking me to the country school where she taught. She made the decision to take me after I would not stop crying every day for a month when she left me with Mrs. Travis, my babysitter, who collected two dollars a week for keeping me. Frustrated with the situation, Mama made a few calculations and decided she could save the money she was paying Mrs. Travis and also save her child from daily heartbreak by taking me to work with her.

On the day she took my hand and we walked together past my baby sitter house to the bus stop on Whitfield Mills Road, I began my career as a schoolgirl. Even at that early age, I felt I belonged in a classroom. From my point of view, I was part of Mama's class and the big kids from grades one through six had better get used to me. Without a choice, those school children did get used to me, especially after I showed them that I could read as well as some of the third graders by the time I reached my third birthday. Like those country scholars, as Mama called them, I did my homework every day.

My sisters took delight in helping me, as well as in ridiculing my pitiful efforts sometimes. Whatever their motives, my sisters gave me plenty of attention. They set high standards for my performance.

Having my own school to attend was the greatest thing in my world, even though my school wasn't made of red bricks like the city school my sisters attended. It certainly never bothered me that Mama's schoolhouse, known as Cone Hill Community School, was a one-room unpainted shack covered with graying and splintery boards. I never thought my school wasn't grand because it sat in a dusty clearing surrounded by pine trees. Only in retrospect can I see that Cone Hill School was actually a fragile, worn-out building with broken steps and a leaky roof. However, to a two-year-old, this place for learning was a magical place at the end of a magical path which extended from Shiloh Road, where the bus let me and Mama off, to the schoolhouse door. So, we had to walk about a quarter of a mile to our special place of books and ideas. I remember many days when I would kick a rock from the big road to the school building while counting all the way up to a hundred, then up to two hundred, and eventually up to one thousand.

As previously noted, by the time I was three years old, due to intense exposure to written language at school and at home, I could read almost any text whether I understood the meanings of the words or not; and I was scribbling in tablets and on walls on a regular basis. I became a show-off for adult company, and I reveled in all the compliments grown-ups gave me for demonstrating good reading and writing abilities at such a young age.

One proud moment I still remember vividly from this early period of my life occurred one spring morning while Mama and I were waiting for the public bus that would take us to Cone Hill School. It was one of those clear, crisp new mornings that poets immortalize in song. The warm sunshine was a welcome change from the cold haze that had paled our winter travels to school, which began at 6:30 A. M.

At sunrise on that glorious day, I was in love with the green grass and miniature wild flowers that checkered the bank where we stood waiting. I was so happy that I started to dance and sing out loud. I sang all about Billy Boy and his remarkable cherry pie-baking wife; I sang about a soldier boy who was unkind to a doting girl; and I sang about a careless pussycat falling into a well.

When an old man, who was my accidental audience, began to clap, I suddenly became aware of myself as an uncommon spectacle and felt embarrassed. But then he expressed pleasure in my performance, and he told my mother that I was a pretty smart little girl.

With the flourish of a magician, the old man reached inside his pocket and came out with a shiny silver dime. He presented it to me, saying I deserved a prize for knowing so much to sing about. Of course, today I realize I provided a minor amusement for an old man who may have remembered what it had been like to be young in springtime; and such a reverie may have prompted a small gesture of generosity on his part.

But for me, at that tender age, the dime the old man gave me was a very meaningful reward. One important lesson I learned from receiving the gift was: knowledge is important and smart people will be admired even by strangers.

During the time I was an active member of Mama's class, I observed that my mother was a wonderful teacher. She knew just how to interest and encourage children of all ages, from three to seventeen—the ages of the youngest and oldest of her pupils at Cone Hill School. All the scholars loved their teacher, Mrs. Lola Smith. She never had to whip them to get them to behave.

Like all the other students in Mama's class, I copied lessons from the board and raised my hand to ask Mrs. Smith for permission. Because of the seriousness of my endeavor to conform and perform, I was given my own set of books and notebooks. But being cooperative in the classroom was not the main reason I learned to read and scribble so fast. My sisters' meanness deserves most of the credit.

There was a game my sisters used to play between the two of them. Its purpose was to deliberately cut me out of their conversations. My sisters used their higher knowledge of reading and spelling to send messages back and forth between them. The louder I expressed my outrage over the exclusion, the happier they became. As I simmered in the wake of demonstrations of their smug superiority, I plotted to break it down. I started to remember what they spelled out or wrote down, and then I'd get Mama to decode their signs. Once I received the meanings associated with their alphabets and numbers, I would remember and transfer bits of decoded information to new plots from which they designed to exclude me. Of course, Mama was always happy to assist me in thwarting their games. And with her clandestine help, I could tell my sisters, with increasing regularity, the meanings of their notes and verbal codes. When my sisters became convinced that they could not spell out messages over my head, they stopped trying. But, by that time, they had taught me some valuable phonics lessons.

From the time I learned to read, I read everything I could find on my level. Mama's classroom had lots of picture books and textbooks she purchased herself, using money from her small salary. But I soon went through them all. I borrowed my sisters' books whenever they were willing to give them up, and I always wanted access to more. After my father discovered my keen interest in books, he began bringing them home from his school. And, he purchased a set of World Book Encyclopedias for our home.

As a young child, I especially loved fairy tales and rhymes about naughty animals and children—the naughtier the better. The beauty and the horror of the world of make-believe made me a dreamer. During my preadolescence, I loved to imagine myself as the storybook heroine who would come to a good end after undeserved suffering.

The pace of my reading accelerated when, at the age of ten, I discovered the public library for Negroes in Jackson. The library was about three miles from my home. And walking there meant traveling through a white neighborhood sandwiched between two black neighborhoods. The white stretch, which was about a mile long, was dangerous. But, through practice, I figured out how to avoid the puppies that would race out of well-kept yards to snip at my heels, and I learned to dodge pebbles certain little white children would throw at me.

During school breaks, I tried my walk to the Negro library at different times in the afternoon, and I figured out the best times to pass through the long white mile. Still, whenever I approached a bad strip of houses, I would walk really fast and then slow down when I entered safer areas. I made this solo journey twice every week during school vacations and every Saturday when school was in session. Neither summer heat nor winter chill deterred me from going to the library to return books I had read or to check out precious new books. I filled my life with Heidi, Mary Poppins, Little Women, Huck Finn, and Pippi Longstockings.

Then in seventh grade, upon my English teacher's recommendation, I read Richard Wright's *Black Boy*. It was then that I began to lose my taste for romance. I began to brood over more serious texts and to pay attention to the news, which was filled with racial issues and racial violence occurring in Mississippi and all across the South. Songs of sorrow and true stories of inhumanity invaded my very soul. The summer after I turned eleven I cried for Emmett Till when I learned that he, a Northern colored child of thirteen, while visiting his cousins in Money, Mississippi, had been brutally murdered for not knowing he had to keep the face of humility in the store where he purchased candy from a white woman. I felt vulnerable to pain, but I was sure I was meant to survive. I feared more for my family and circle of friends than for myself. And my worst fear seemed to come true several years later when my neighbor and civil rights hero, Medgar Evers, was shot down in his own yard. At that point, the whole world seemed like a dark and foreboding place.

The outrages put into focus by the civil rights protests of the sixties descended upon my "darkling plain." Like Matthew Arnold, the poet to whom I allude, I was bewildered by the cruel realities of the world—the part darkly colored by racism. While my fantasy idols crumpled and died, I sought understanding through history books and biographies. I read books and essays by Frederick Douglass, and I learned about the Jewish Holocaust by reading Anne Frank. I read books such as *The Grapes of Wrath, Of Mice and Men, and To Kill A Mockingbird.*

Ironically, from stories of such harsh realities I was able to have my faith in humanity restored. I was heartened by the resiliency of characters, who, in the face of trouble, were buoyed by the triumph of good over evil. I began to see the sufferings of such protagonists, with whom I vicariously shared adventures, as catalysts for a better world. My faith in justice and karma became stronger as I learned to do whatever I could to please the universe and to maintain myself by not falling apart in the face of temporary chaos.

Today, I enjoy all types of books, from humor to murder mysteries to gothic tales. I even read political tracts because I like to weigh different ideas and ideologies and then discover what I believe. I like the feel of ordering my ideas into texts, but I try not to take myself so seriously that criticism will devastate me. I try to tell the truth always laced with humor.

www.ingramcontent.com/pod-product-compliance
Lightning Source LLC
LaVergne TN
LVHW051508070426
835507LV00022B/2988